WHAT YOU NEED TO KNOW

TWENTY QUESTIONS
AND ANSWERS ABOUT

Climate Change

Sally Ride Science

CLIMATE CENTRAL

An innovative science
education company

Sound science
& vibrant media

**The team at Sally Ride
Science includes** Sally Ride,
Tam O'Shaughnessy, Karen Flammer,
Wes Brumitt, Chris Leong,
Brenda Wilson, Stacey Klaman,
Erin Hunter, Monnee Tong, and
many others.

**The team at Climate Central
includes** Michael Lemonick,
Remik Ziemlinski, Jessica Harrop,
Berrien Moore III, Heidi Cullen,
Eric Larson, Ben Strauss,
Claudia Tebaldi, Nicole Heller,
and Phil Duffy.

Published by Sally Ride Science
www.SallyRideScience.com
Sally Ride Science is a trademark of Imaginary Lines, Inc.
Sally Ride Science, 9191 Towne Centre Drive, Suite L101, San Diego, CA 92122

Book Design: Steve Curtis Design

ISBN: 978-1-933798-40-0

First Edition
Printed in United States of America
10 9 8 7 6 5 4 3 2 1

*Sally Ride Science and Climate Central are committed to minimizing their environmental impact
by using ecologically sound practices. Let's all do our part to create a healthier planet.*

*These pages are printed on paper made with 100% recycled fiber, 50% post-consumer waste,
bleached without chlorine, and manufactured using 100% renewable energy.*

Contents

Introduction

Scientists and policymakers overwhelmingly agree that Earth's climate is changing. They agree that human activities are largely to blame, among them the burning of fossil fuels for transportation, manufacturing, and the production of electricity; the widespread destruction of forests; and the practice of large-scale agriculture. They also agree that the consequences, including rising sea levels; disruptions to water supplies; increases in wildfires, droughts, and severe storms; and the acidification of the oceans are underway now, and could be harmful to people, animals, plants, and the worldwide economy.

Such changes are in addition to the natural variations in climate, which are a hallmark of our planet. A further hallmark of Earth is that its human society is rapidly developing a deep scientific understanding of the climate system. Moreover, this scientific understanding is being assessed carefully every five to six years through the processes of the Intergovernmental Panel on Climate Change (www.ipcc.ch). This assessment looks not only at the underlying science, but it also assesses our knowledge on ways to address climate change.

The first way to address climate change is mitigation—limiting future emissions of greenhouse gases by (to name just one possible strategy) switching from carbon-intensive fuels like coal to renewable sources of energy and by reducing our use of energy through smart conservation. The second is adaptation, or adjusting to changes in climate (moving people away from sea coasts, perhaps).

In order to decide what actions to take, however, it's crucial to have the best possible information on what we actually know for sure about climate change and its projected effects. How much, exactly, will sea level rise, and how quickly? How much warmer will temperatures be in 50 years? In 100? How well can we predict what areas will be hit by droughts? What steps require international cooperation, and what can be accomplished at the national, local, and even personal level? And how much will it cost?

This book represents a joint effort between the scientists and communicators at Climate Central and Sally Ride Science. Using straightforward language, we divide the issue of climate change into three parts—The Science, The Impacts, and The Solutions. In part one, we present an overview of what scientists know about the nature of climate change. In part two, we present the likely impacts of climate change and what could be in store in the future.

And in part three, we review a range of possible solutions. We hope that this approach enables readers to better see the ever-growing risks associated with climate change and better know what solutions are available to them. Climate change is a problem, by its very nature, that will require a long-term strategy.

Everything you read in this book is based on the best scientific data and understanding available to date. Like all branches of science, the study of climate change will keep absorbing new data and reaching new insights. But we emphasize that while we don't know everything about climate change by any means, we do know a great deal—much more than we did just two decades ago when the issue first emerged. We know enough to state with a high degree of confidence that human-caused climate change will be one of the greatest challenges of the coming century, and that addressing it calls for an honest discussion of the science, without respect to politics or advocacy of any sort.

We hope this book will contribute to that discussion.

Berrien Moore III, Ph.D.   Sally K. Ride, Ph.D.

Berrien Moore III is the founding director of Climate Central. Before joining Climate Central, Dr. Moore served as Director of the Institute for the Study of Earth, Oceans, and Space at the University of New Hampshire. He also served as coordinating lead author of the final chapter of the *Intergovernmental Panel on Climate Change's Third Assessment Report*.

Sally K. Ride, best known as the first American woman to fly in space, is President and Chief Executive Officer of Sally Ride Science and Emerita Professor of Physics at the University of California, San Diego. She is also co-author of *Mission Planet Earth*, an introduction to the Earth and the changes taking place in its climate.

What is the *greenhouse effect*?

An ordinary greenhouse keeps plants warm in winter without using a heater. It works because the Sun's rays shine through the glass walls and roof, warming the inside—and that same glass keeps the heat from escaping.

The greenhouse effect warms the Earth (and other planets) in a similar way, although it's not exactly the same. The Earth's transparent atmosphere lets sunlight through to warm the ground and the oceans (more when it's clear, less when it's cloudy). The Earth's warmed surface releases some of that heat in the form of infrared radiation—a form of light, but invisible to human eyes.

This infrared light wants to keep on going, right back out into space, taking the warmth with it. But some gases in the atmosphere—most importantly carbon dioxide, or CO_2, but also methane, nitrous oxide, and water vapor—won't let all the infrared radiation pass through. These

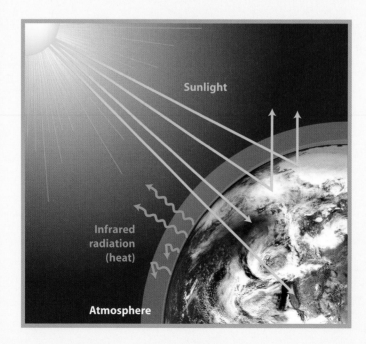

The Greenhouse Effect The greenhouse effect happens when sunlight warms the Earth, and molecules in the atmosphere intercept the resulting heat before it can escape to space.

"greenhouse gases" are very good at absorbing infrared light. They spread the heat back to the land and the oceans. So greenhouse gases act sort of (though not exactly) like the glass in the greenhouse. They let sunlight through on its way in from space, but intercept some of the infrared light on its way back out.

As a result, the lower part of the atmosphere stays much warmer than it would otherwise. Greenhouse gases are a natural part of Earth's atmosphere, and it's a good thing they are! Without them, the average surface temperature of the Earth would be about 33°C (60°F) lower than it is now, and life as we know it would be impossible. On the other hand, Venus has a much thicker atmosphere than Earth, most of it CO_2, and the surface temperature there is above 444°C (800°F). Part of that is because Venus is closer to the Sun, but almost 389°C (700°F) of it is a result of Venus' powerful greenhouse effect.

Climate scientists know how the natural greenhouse effect works on Earth and other planets. That's why they worry about what is happening as humans change the balance of greenhouse gases, for example by burning fossil fuels that release more CO_2 to the air than what is released naturally.

How do we know?

One important way is from satellite data. Space provides an ideal environment to measure the Earth's energy budget—the amount of energy coming in versus the amount of energy going out. For the energy coming in, we use sensors such as the Total Solar Irradiance Sensor, which first flew on NASA's Solar Radiation and Climate Experiment. It will be continued on the National Polar-orbiting Operational Environmental Satellite System, or NPOESS. For the energy going out we use sensors such as CERES, which stands for Clouds and the Earth's Radiant Energy System, flying on NASA's Earth Observing System. CERES will also be continued on NPOESS.

Q

What is the difference between *global warming* and *climate change*?

A

Depending on who's talking, there can be an enormous difference between *global warming* and *climate change*—or no difference at all.

A lot of people, including many journalists who write about the topic, use the two terms interchangeably. When reporters first began doing stories back in the late 1980s about how humans seemed to be doing things that result in heating up the planet, the term they usually used was *global warming*. That's because the basic effect of greenhouse gases like carbon dioxide is to do exactly that. They trap more and more of the

Sun's energy and drive the average temperature of the planet upward.

But that's only one dimension of the issue. Average temperature is global. Climate is local, and involves not just average temperature, but also other factors that vary, such as humidity, cloudiness, rain (or snow), how this precipitation is spread throughout the year (does it mostly come in one short burst, or over a rainy season, or evenly all year long, or something in between?). If you live by the sea, ocean currents also make a difference. London, England, is farther north than Montreal,

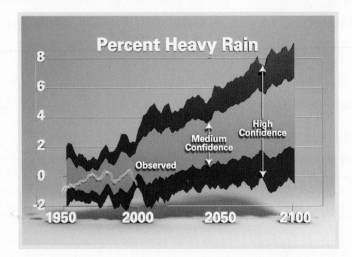

The percentage of days with heavy rainfall somewhere in the continental U.S. has risen, and is likely to keep rising.

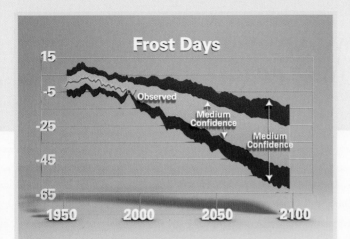

Frost Days

Observed

Medium Confidence

Medium Confidence

1950   2000   2050   2100

Warming temperatures will mean fewer days of frost across the continental U.S. as the century progresses.

Canada, for example but it has much milder winters, because the Gulf Stream carries warm water across the Atlantic to keep it relatively balmy.

Scientists have learned that raising the Earth's temperature is very likely to change many of these factors. So while global warming is what's causing it, what most people are going to notice is not necessarily warming but rather a change in climate.

There's one more factor. Some people want to emphasize the potentially serious consequences of the problem. Others want to convince everyone to think that it's not such a big deal, or that humans aren't really causing the problem in the first place. So they choose one term or the other because they think it sounds more or less scary. But since nobody can agree about which term actually is scarier,

both groups use both terms at different times.

That sounds pretty confusing. The bottom line is that while *global warming* isn't wrong, *climate change* more accurately describes what's happening. That's a major reason that many people have settled on the latter term.

But most of the time, whether people use *global warming* or *climate change*, they're almost certainly talking about the same thing.

How do we know?

Scientists have identified no fewer than 44 essential climate variables—including not only global temperature but also clouds, precipitation, snow cover, ice cover, sea level, and even biological activity. Many of these are measured from space, with satellites including the U.S./Japanese Tropical Rainfall Measuring Mission, which looks at precipitation; NASA's ICESAT Mission, which measures the extent and elevation of ice; and the U.S./French *TOPEX* and *Jason* satellites, which keep track of sea level.

Q
How do we know it's not a natural cycle?

A

If the Earth's temperature had been steady for millions of years and only started rising in the past half century or so, the answer would be obvious.

But the temperature hasn't been steady at all. Twenty thousand years ago, the planet was going through an ice age, with glaciers covering much of Europe and North America. A hundred million years ago, the Earth was so warm that crocodile-like creatures prowled through tropical vegetation not far from the North Pole.

In other words, climate variations aren't at all unusual. So how do we know this one is caused by humans?

Several reasons. First, we know that burning coal, oil, and gas releases heat-trapping carbon dioxide, or CO_2. And we know, thanks to careful measurements that started in the late 1950s, that carbon dioxide levels in the atmosphere have been steadily climbing as we burn more. Not only that— chemists can tell the difference between the CO_2 released naturally by plants and animals and the CO_2 from burning fossil fuels. About a quarter of the CO_2 now in the atmosphere is the result of human activity.

The one obvious natural suspect—the Sun—can pretty

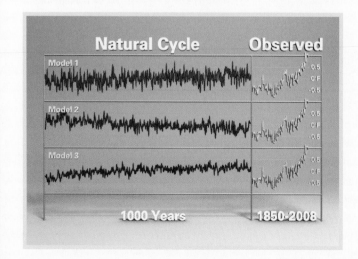

When scientists look at climate variations in the past, they don't see anything like today's warming.

3

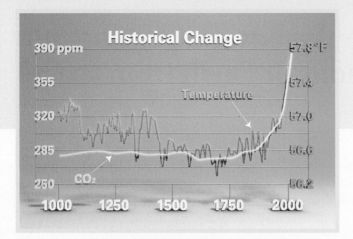

Historical Change

390 ppm · 57.8 °F

355 · 57.4

Temperature

320 · 57.0

285 · 56.6

250 · 56.2

CO₂

1000 · 1250 · 1500 · 1750 · 2000

Carbon dioxide (measured in parts per million, or ppm—the number of carbon dioxide molecules in 1 million molecules of air) and temperature have been rising almost in lockstep—a clue that it's not natural.

much be ruled out. It's an obvious suspect because astronomers know that the Sun can vary in brightness. When it does, the amount of heat it sends to the Earth varies too. It wouldn't take much brightening to cause the increases in temperature we've seen. But satellites have been monitoring the Sun since the 1970s—when the fastest warming has been taking place—and the brightening just isn't there.

There's plenty of other evidence—the pattern of warming, for example, which is greatest in the Arctic, and the pace, which is faster (as best we can tell) than prehistoric warming episodes. The upper atmosphere has actually cooled, because so much heat has been trapped below.

The bottom line is that nobody has come up with a natural explanation for the current warming episode that fits the observations. At the same time, the un-natural explanation—that our industrial civilization is a big part of the cause—fits the evidence.

That's how we know it isn't natural. One last thing. If the Earth has survived earlier warming episodes, what's so bad about this one even if it *isn't* natural? The problem is that our civilization— where cities are located, where we grow food, where we get fresh water—is all based on the climate we've experienced for the last 10,000 years. So are many of the world's ecosystems. If the climate changes, many of those things will suddenly find themselves in the wrong place.

How do we know?

Two NASA satellites, known as *ACE* and *STEREO*, measure the brightness of the Sun from Earth orbit, where the dimming effects of our atmosphere are minimal. Another satellite, called *Aqua*, looks down with an instrument called AIRS at the atmosphere from above to measure how much carbon dioxide is in it. And, as we discussed in the answer to the first question, we are measuring the Earth's radiation budget from space.

Q

A

What are the advantages of observations of Earth from space?

Observations of the Earth from space provide a unique vantage point for gathering information essential to forecasting the weather, assessing environmental hazards, managing natural resources, and improving our understanding of climate. Since the first satellites carried cameras into orbit in the late 1950s, space observations have added a matchless perspective, which has grown richer as our space-based instruments have evolved in terms of both variety and sophistication.

Ground, sea, and air-based observing systems that contribute to monitoring our planet are also

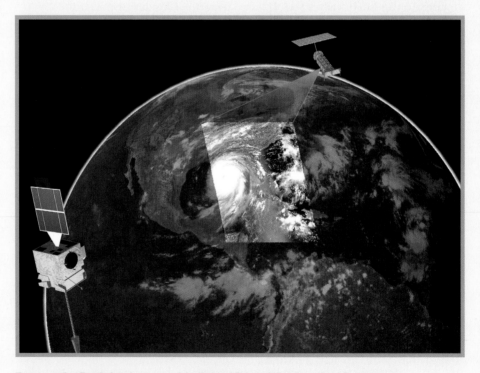

Eyes on the Earth Artist's concept of the National Polar-orbiting Operational Environmental Satellite System, which is part of the U.S.'s plan to increase monitoring of climate and weather from space. The two big advantages of space-based observations are the ability to look at huge areas all at once, and the ability to see places like the middle of the ocean, where measurements were once hard to come by.

very important. But they have a major limitation—their view is limited. Even though each piece of surface-based data can be combined into large maps, the data represents only the conditions at one location. Beyond that, while surface observations are relatively numerous in many parts of the world, they are sparse in others— much of Africa, parts of South America, and the oceans. From space, by contrast, you can see the full picture.

For example, sensors on Earth observation satellites measure rainfall and cloud cover, the chemistry and temperature of the atmosphere, water levels in lakes and reservoirs, and deforestation around the planet. More importantly, because satellites orbit the planet for years, they can make consistent measurements over long periods of time. That's how we know so confidently that sea level really is rising, that ice shelves keep breaking off Antarctica, that

rainforests are disappearing in the Amazon (and just how quickly), and that Greenland is shedding more ice into the sea than it gains in new snowfall (and, once again, how quickly).

Earth observation satellites also gave us the first global look at the most fundamental climate measurement—how much energy from the Sun hits the Earth and how much energy leaves the Earth. Scientists perform these measurements by pointing a sensor at the Sun to measure incoming solar irradiance and by pointing a sensor at the Earth to measure the energy that is being re-radiated outward. Other sensors measure properties that influence how much solar energy stays in the Earth's atmosphere as a result of cloud cover (a major influence). They also measure various gases, ocean currents, and wind patterns.

Space is truly an ideal vantage point for monitoring our planet's climate.

Is there disagreement among scientists about climate change? Is it caused by humans?

The U.S. National Academy of Sciences has declared that climate change is occurring and that humans are very likely causing it. So have the scientific societies of China, France, Germany, India, Japan, Russia, Brazil, the United Kingdom, and many other countries.

The Intergovernmental Panel on Climate Change, or IPCC, a body made up of hundreds of experts from scores of countries, issued their most recent report, the Fourth Assessment Report, in 2007, saying that "warming of the climate system is unequivocal." The IPCC periodically assembles peer-reviewed research on climate science into an overall picture. Representatives from member countries, including the U.S., negotiate the wording of the final report line by line. The most recent report says, "Most of the observed increase in global average temperatures since the mid-20th century is very likely due to the observed increase in anthropogenic GHG [human greenhouse gas] concentrations."

More recently, in June 2009, the U.S. Global Change Research Program, which is a joint scientific venture of 13 federal agencies and the White House, released the results of a multiyear study. This study, like many others, found that "the global warming observed over the past 50 years is due primarily to human-induced emissions of heat-trapping gases. These emissions come mainly from the burning of fossil fuels (coal, oil, and gas), with important contributions from the clearing of forests, agricultural practices, and other activities."

Therefore, the overwhelming scientific consensus is that climate change is real, that it is being caused by human actions, and that there will be potentially significant impacts for people around the globe.

Climate scientists continue their research to increase knowledge on many aspects of climate change, including predictions about how quickly temperatures are likely to rise, what impact melting glaciers will have on sea level, and whether hurricanes will increase in quantity or intensity. Such information is essential if we are to wisely and effectively mitigate the potential impacts of climate change.

The climate system is extraordinarily complex. Understanding it is a grand scientific challenge—it is also an immensely important one.

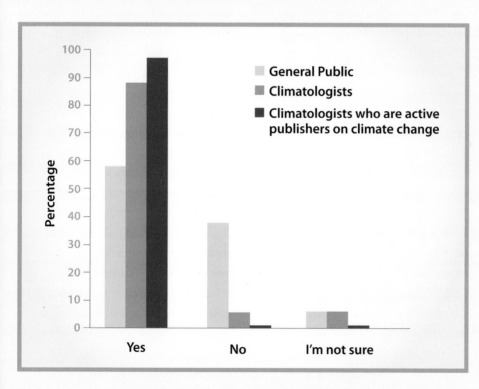

Are Humans Changing the Temperature of the Earth?
A recent study asked this question of the public, of climate scientists who don't publish many papers, and of those who do.

Q We've had a cold winter. Does that mean the overall trend for global warming is over?

A No. Weather conditions at specific locations, including temperature, are dynamic and vary with regional and hemispheric weather patterns. The average global air temperature, which is the sum of regional temperatures, has been gradually rising over the past 100 years. According to NASA, the ten warmest years on record have occurred since 1997. *The Fourth Assessment of the Intergovernmental Panel on Climate Change*, or IPCC, reported in 2007 that 11 out of 12 of the years from 1995 to 2006—the exception being 1996—are 11 of the 12 warmest years since 1850.

Despite the current global warming trend, it is important to remember that not all parts of the Earth warm equally or at the same rate. The Arctic, for example, is warming faster than other areas, while the equatorial region is warming much more slowly. In fact, the Arctic is warming so fast that some climate modelers project an ice-free Arctic Ocean in summertime—possibly as early as 2040, but very likely by end of the century—if emissions of greenhouse gases continue to grow at current rates.

For periods of a few years, regional weather patterns can dominate local temperatures, masking a general upward trend in global temperatures. For example, suppose that the world's average temperature rises a fraction of a degree in a given year. The prevailing winds where you live might shift into a pattern that could actually make the winter in your area several degrees colder than normal.

Even the worldwide trend is not a smoothly rising line, but rather a signal that fluctuates, as shown in the graph above. Over a short timescale of a couple years, one can expect temperatures actually to fall below the average value, even though over a longer timescale the average is still rising. There is, as one would expect, natural variability within the overall trend.

6

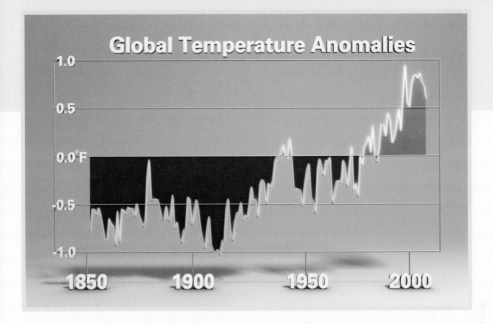

Global Temperature Anomalies

1.0

0.5

0.0°F

-0.5

-1.0

1850   1900   1950   2000

Global warming isn't a straight line—there are ups and downs. But the overall trend is unmistakably upward.

An example of the dynamic nature of climate variability was evident in 1998 when the average temperature lurched upward significantly (more than .72°C [1.3°F]). It turned out that the Pacific El Niño current was especially strong that year. Afterward, temperatures actually dropped a bit for the next couple of years.

So, while measurements show that the average temperature of the planet has risen over the past century and likely will keep rising over the next 100 years, we should not expect every year to be warmer than the year before at every spot on the Earth. In some places, and even for the Earth as a whole, there may be years when it's actually a little cooler than the previous year. Nevertheless, the data indicates that over the long term, we're heading toward a hotter world—a reality that is further supported by our knowledge of the relationship between carbon dioxide, or CO_2, and other greenhouse gases and temperature, as well as our knowledge of the climate system.

Plants need CO_2 to live. So isn't more of it a good thing?

We do not yet know enough to make adequate projections of the global trends for plant life in a world with higher levels of carbon dioxide, or CO_2. It is clear, however, that there can be both positive and negative responses.

One of the first things taught in biology class is that animals breathe in oxygen and exhale CO_2, while plants take in CO_2 during the day and release oxygen. In a process called "photosynthesis," plants use the energy in sunlight to convert CO_2 and water to sugar and oxygen. The plants use the sugar for food—food that we use, too, when we eat plants or animals that have eaten plants—and they release the oxygen into the atmosphere. If it weren't for plants, we'd have no oxygen in our air!

So, if we're putting more CO_2 into the atmosphere by burning fossil fuels, you might expect plants to grow better. But the story is not quite that simple. When biologists have grown crops like wheat, soybeans, and rice inside greenhouses with extra CO_2 present, the plants have indeed grown more rapidly and more abundantly. For the past several years, scientists all over the world have also been doing a series of experiments called "Free-Air Concentration Enrichment," or FACE. Instead of using greenhouses, they grow crops in open fields to give them the most natural environment possible and pump in extra CO_2 from a network of pipes.

The results of these experiments have shown that the crops do not thrive as well in this environment. Plants do need CO_2, but they also need water, nitrogen, and other nutrients. Increase one of these without increasing the others and there's a limit to how much the plants will benefit. Some don't grow much more at all. Others, like wheat, grow bigger but end up with less nitrogen. As a result, insects end up eating more to get the nitrogen they need. The nutritional value of food plants would be similarly reduced for other animals—including humans. Also, we could end up with vegetables that have too much carbon—perhaps producing spinach that would be very tough to chew!

Simulating a High-Carbon World In the Free-Air Concentration Enrichment experiment, scientists pump extra CO_2 into natural environments.

Q If we can't predict weather two weeks ahead, how can we predict climate fifty years from now?

A

Climate refers to the average environmental conditions in a particular place over time, usually over a 30-year span. *Weather* describes the *actual* conditions at a given time, day-to-day, and even hour-to-hour.

There are plenty of other familiar situations where the same sort of difference applies. For example, we know the average lifespan of people born in the U.S., but individuals live a lot longer or a lot shorter than the average, depending on their diets, lifestyles, genetics, and other factors.

The difference between average conditions and actual conditions is why weather reports include two numbers—the normal, or *average*, high for the day, which is climate; and the *actual* high for the day, which is weather, or at least one aspect of weather.

The reason it's so hard to predict the weather very far in advance is because weather is incredibly complex and dynamic. Factors like today's temperature, humidity, prevailing winds, and local geography all have

an influence on tomorrow's weather. What happens tomorrow determines what will happen the next day, and so on. Even the tiniest unknown factor in today's weather, say the humidity over a patch of forest, increases the uncertainty of making tomorrow's forecast. The situation makes the forecasts for next week even less certain, and forecasting even further into the future becomes increasingly more challenging.

Climate is very different. While climate is also an exceedingly complex system, we aren't looking at local, day-to-day details, but rather focusing on the average conditions for a region over time. And those change much more slowly. Nobody can tell you what the temperature will be on August 10, 2020, in New York City, but it's very likely to be a lot warmer than on February 10, 2020, because New York City's climate is hot in summer and cold in winter. The city also happens to have a fair amount of both rain and snow. The climate in San Diego, California, is warm, but not hot most of the year, with

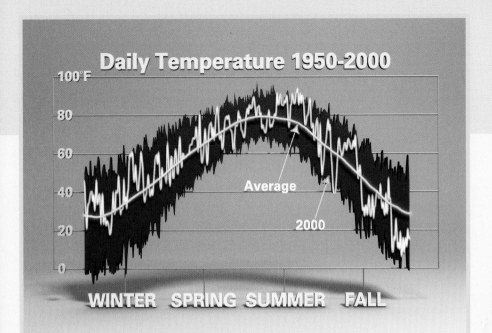

Daily Temperature 1950-2000

WINTER SPRING SUMMER FALL

The dark blue band (all years) and the light blue line show how rarely the actual temperature hits the average.

relatively little rain and essentially no snow. Buffalo, New York, is very cold in winter and gets a huge amount of snow. And so on. You instinctively know the climate where you live because it doesn't change a lot from year to year.

There are many factors that determine climate, including the Earth's orbit around the Sun and the Sun's brightness. Climate is also governed by changes in ice sheets, in ocean currents, and in the gases that make up the atmosphere. Climate scientists continue to use Earth observations and models to improve their understanding of these forces. They now have decades of environmental data and model experience to know in a general way what's likely to happen if one of those factors changes. As a consequence, it is possible to project with some confidence—while acknowledging the uncertainties—what the climate will be like 50 years in the future based on general trends; on computer models that capture, though not perfectly, the dynamics of the climate system; and on our scientific insights into past climate conditions.

Q Is global warming making hurricanes worse?

There is no simple answer to this question. That's partly because you have to define what you mean by "worse." You might be asking whether we're seeing more hurricanes than we did in the past. Or you might be asking if individual hurricanes are getting stronger. Or you might be asking if we're seeing more damage from hurricanes.

Then, once you know what the question really is, you have to figure out what role climate change might be playing in each of these.

At the most basic level, most hurricane experts agree that warming ocean waters should, on average, make hurricanes more powerful. That's because hurricanes get their energy from the evaporation of seawater—and seawater evaporates more easily when it's warmer.

It's for this reason that the Intergovernmental Panel on Climate Change, or IPCC, the most authoritative climate-change group in the world, projects that there will be a "likely increase in tropical cyclone intensity" for the coming century, thanks to human-caused global warming. (The term *hurricane* is only used for Atlantic storms; *tropical cyclone* covers hurricane-like storms in all parts of the world).

Is it already happening? Possibly. There are hints in the data that suggest an increase in the number of hurricanes in the North Atlantic over the past few decades. The evidence is better for an increase in hurricane intensity. But in both cases, more data are needed before scientists can be certain.

Beyond that, while most climate models predict that the strongest tropical cyclones will get stronger as human-caused global warming continues (that's why the word *likely* in the IPCC's statement), some models suggest that the number of storms may not increase. Many factors influence the formation of hurricanes and tropical cyclones, including wind patterns, ocean currents, and local weather conditions. All of these may change in a warming world, in ways scientists aren't yet certain of. So it's really hard to project how the numbers will change worldwide.

There could be more hurricanes and tropical storms in the future. Or there could actually be fewer. This is a difficult problem and more data and research are needed.

If we're talking about damage, though, everyone agrees that it will get worse. Part of that will be due to global warming. Warming makes sea level higher, which means the kind of storm surges that devastated New Orleans during Hurricane Katrina will have a head start.

But a more important factor in the near term is likely to be population growth in low-lying countries like Bangladesh and near seacoasts in places like Florida, Texas, and Louisiana. We've already seen that kind of growth over the past couple of decades, putting tens or even hundreds of millions more people in harm's way. Even a relatively mild hurricane can kill more people and destroy more property than the most powerful storm could have 50 years ago. So while Hurricane Katrina, for example, was the most damaging storm to hit the U.S. on record, it wasn't the most powerful.

It just happened to strike a major population center whose hurricane-protection system wasn't up to the job.

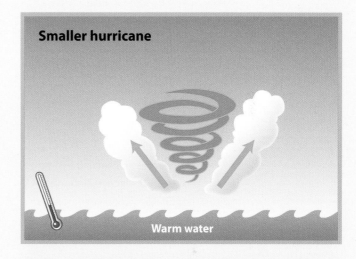

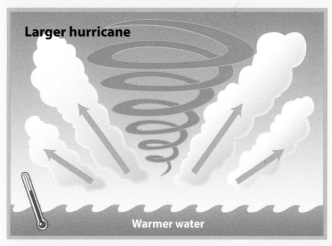

Heating Up Hurricanes Hurricanes get their energy from the evaporation of warm seawater (top). If the sea surface gets warmer, there's more energy available to make the storms more powerful (bottom).

Q What could the effects of climate change be?

A Scientists now believe that the Earth could warm up by as much as 3.9°C (7°F), on average, by the end of the century, if emissions of greenhouse gases continue to grow at current rates. That could trigger all sorts of big changes in the environment.

To start with, scientists expect sea level to rise by three feet or more—partly because water expands as it warms, partly due to melting ice in Greenland and other places. Low-lying areas— significant parts of states like Florida, and entire countries like Bangladesh and the Maldives will be more prone to erosion and to catastrophic flooding.

The warming could also make the most powerful of tropical storms even more powerful. And rainstorms in general are likely to become more intense, with more of them causing damaging floods.

As mountain glaciers melt, they'll cause even more flooding— at first. But if they shrink enough, the fresh water they provide will become scarce. Billions of people in India and China, for example, depend on water that comes off glaciers in the Himalayas and the Tibetan Plateau. In the U.S., earlier snowmelt in the Rocky and Sierra Nevada mountains will mean less meltwater for a thirsty California during the summer when it is really needed.

In already arid regions like Australia and the American West, droughts are likely to come more often and be more severe. That's likely to lead to more wildfires. Heat waves will be more frequent too, in temperate zones, including most of the continental U.S.

All of these changes would affect people's comfort and their physical safety. But they could have an even greater impact on other species. Plants and animals thrive in specific climate conditions and cannot easily adapt to rapid changes.

The trees that produce Vermont maple syrup, for example, may have trouble surviving in Vermont as the New England climate changes, and Georgia may lose its population of Brown Thrashers—the state bird.

	+ 1–2° F	+ 3–5° F	+ 6–7° F
Coral Reef Bleaching	Coral bleaching events in about 1/6 of the world's reefs	Most coral reefs bleached world wide	Widespread coral mortality
Biological Extinctions	Amphibian extinctions	20–30% of species extinct	Extinction of up to 40% of species
Coastal Impacts	Increased damage from floods and storms	Millions more people could experience coastal flooding each year	Greater than 30% of global coastal wetlands lost
	2010	2030–2060	2070–2100

Escalating Risk
As temperatures increase through the coming century, so will the damage.

The warming of the oceans has already contributed to a worldwide die-off in coral reefs, which is expected to accelerate. Corals are home to a wide variety of sea-dwelling creatures, so when they go, many other species could be in big trouble—including the fish people in places like the Philippines depend on for income and for food.

If we cut back drastically on greenhouse gases, we can limit how high the temperature will go. But if not, these changes will continue to happen—and the further they go, the harder they'll be to reverse.

How do we know?

We know ice is disappearing into the sea thanks in part to a pair of satellites. Collectively called *GRACE*, their separation changes slightly as they pass over areas of higher and lower gravity, representing higher and lower mass. Over time, they've seen Greenland getting less massive as it loses old ice faster than it is gaining new ice.

How big a difference could a few degrees make?

As these words are being written, the temperature outside is 7.2°C (45°F)—a cool, late-winter day in New Jersey. Would it make a huge difference if it were 11°C (52°F)? Probably not—people might just unzip their jackets a little. Similarly, plenty of people wouldn't feel a dramatic difference between 30°C (87°F) and 34°C (94°F) in midsummer—for a day or two, anyway.

Yet an average increase of 3.9°C (7°F) year-round and worldwide—more in some places, less in others—by the end of this century could cause significant impacts. Climate scientists think such an increase in temperature is most likely to come about given current trends in greenhouse gas emissions. They have determined that a temperature change of that magnitude would be enough to threaten coastal cities with rising seas; reduce freshwater availability in the western U.S., India, and many other places; turn some rich farmland arid; and force animals, insects—and the diseases they carry—and hundreds of millions of people to search for new places to live.

Even with just the .56°C (1°F) change that's already occurred, we're seeing a range of impacts around the globe. Many birds now head south for the winter several weeks later than they did a few decades ago, and return earlier—just one of many examples of how ecosystems are being disrupted. The oceans only have to rise a few more feet above their average 2-mile depth before low-lying coastal areas in North Carolina, Florida, and the Gulf Coast will be threatened. Heat waves in places like Phoenix, Arizona, are bad enough already; crank up the temperature by 3.9°C (7°F), and they'll be close to unendurable. Wildfires in the American West are on the rise. There is a long list of impacts when you look at the effect of changing climate conditions, with multiple examples from every state and region.

Higher emissions

Lower emissions

Year: 2010–39 2040–69 2070–99

Higher-emission scenario
Continued reliance on fossil fuels,
causing heat-trapping emissions to rise
Lower-emission scenario
A shift away from fossil fuels in favor
of clean energy, causing heat-trapping
emissions to decline

Summer in the Tri-state Region The tri-state region
(blue) which includes parts of New York, New Jersey, and
Connecticut, could feel like the typical summer in Savannah,
Georgia by the end of the century unless we take action to
reduce heat-trapping emissions today.

Higher emissions

Lower emissions

Year: 2010–39 2040–69 2070–99

Higher-emission scenario
Continued reliance on fossil fuels,
causing heat-trapping emissions to rise
Lower-emission scenario
A shift away from fossil fuels in favor
of clean energy, causing heat-trapping
emissions to decline

Summer in Vermont Vermont (blue) could feel like the
typical summer in Tennessee by the end of the century unless
we take action to reduce heat-trapping emissions today.

27

How much will sea level rise?

There are two main reasons why sea level is rising as the world gets warmer. First, as ice sheets and glaciers melt, they send ice and water pouring into the oceans.

But another reason is that water, like most substances, expands as it heats up—and as greenhouse gases warm the atmosphere, some of that heat is slowly warming the oceans as well.

Scientists understand the expansion of water really well; you can look it up in a textbook. It's much harder to predict what will happen to the ice, though.

It isn't just the melting ice that scientists have to contend with—it's also the fact that tidewater glaciers (glaciers that flow into the sea) and ice sheets move downhill faster with warming. In places like Greenland, that means they drop chunks of ice into the sea at a greater rate than they have in the past—and adding ice to the sea faster than it can melt drives sea level higher. (By contrast, the melting of ice that was in the sea all along, like the ice pack that covers the Arctic Ocean in winter, doesn't make sea level rise at all.

If you have a glass of water with ice cubes in it filled nearly to the top, it doesn't overflow as the ice melts. But dump more ice into that glass and see what happens).

In part because of that uncertainty, and also because of insufficient information about the relationship between melting and sea level in the past, the authoritative Intergovernmental Panel on Climate Change, or IPCC, counted only the expansion of seawater and the increased melting in its latest report. It left the motions of glaciers out entirely. The IPCC knew this could be important, but didn't have enough information to estimate it. Thus, everyone knew that the IPCC's projection that sea level would rise between half a foot and two feet by the end of this century was not the whole story.

Since that report came out in early 2007, though, scientists have gotten a better handle on the uncertainties. They now project that three or four feet of sea-level rise is likely by century's end, if emissions of greenhouse gases continue to grow at current rates.

For millions of people who live in low-lying coastal areas, that's a direct threat.

It's a threat to many millions more because surges of water from storms will push seas even further inland. Coastal marshes tend to absorb the energy of waves and surges. If they disappear under the rising sea, that buffer will be gone, making the land more vulnerable to flooding and erosion. And rising saltwater could get into underground supplies of fresh water. That could threaten drinking-water supplies, disrupt coastal agriculture, and destroy ecosystems. Finally, when heavy rains on land send water gushing down rivers, the rivers will start backing up and flooding low-lying land sooner.

A sea-level rise of three feet might not sound like a lot, but it could do enormous damage.

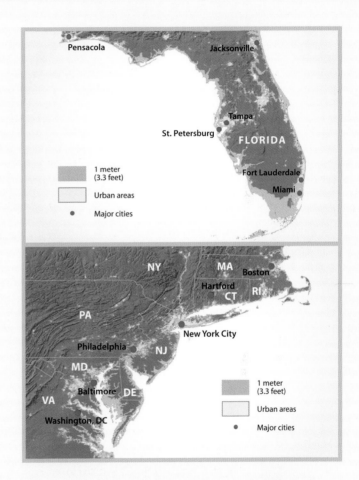

Land Vulnerability To Rising Sea Levels Some coastal areas will become submerged, and storm-driven floods will reach further inland.

How do we know?

The sea surface moves constantly up and down due to tides and ocean waves, but scientists can still measure average sea level to an accuracy of millimeters or less. They do it with satellites, including one called *TOPEX/Poseidon*, and, since 2005, another called *Jason-1* and most recently *Jason-2*. These satellites bounce radar waves off the surface thousands and thousands of times each year, all over the world, to figure out how sea level is changing. Another set of satellites, named *Terra* and *Aqua*, use remote sensors to measure sea surface temperatures.

How do we predict the consequences of climate change?

The Intergovernmental Panel on Climate Change, or IPCC, has not only projected rising temperatures and sea level; it's also made projections about rainfall, growing zones, changes to ecosystems, and more. How can scientists do that?

First, note that they use the word *projection* rather than *prediction*. A projection is an educated guess about the future based on what we know now. It's widely understood that what we know isn't perfect, so a responsible projection will offer a range of outcomes, not a specific prediction.

Even if what we know isn't perfect, we do know a lot. We know the basic physics of the atmosphere. We know how carbon dioxide, or CO_2, and other greenhouse gases trap heat. We know how changes in the brightness of the surface of the Earth—for example, when ice melts to expose rock or water—affect how much sunlight the Earth absorbs. We know how temperature differences between different regions of the Earth force air masses to move around . . . and so on.

We also know, from air bubbles trapped in ancient ice, how CO_2 has affected the Earth's temperature in the past. We know how high sea level was when the Earth was warm enough to melt all the ice on the planet, and how low it was in the depths of the ice ages. We know a lot about the distribution of vegetation during these very different climate regimes. And we know much more accurately than ever what conditions are like today almost everywhere on the planet—temperatures, ice cover, greenhouse gas concentrations, sea level, and more.

When scientists want to project what will happen by 2100, for example, they take all of this information and feed it into global climate models. These are complex computer programs that simulate major parts of the climate system, including the oceans, atmosphere, and land processes. Scientists then test the ability of these models to reproduce actual observations of the present and reconstructed information about the past. Once they see that the models can match observed and historical data, climate

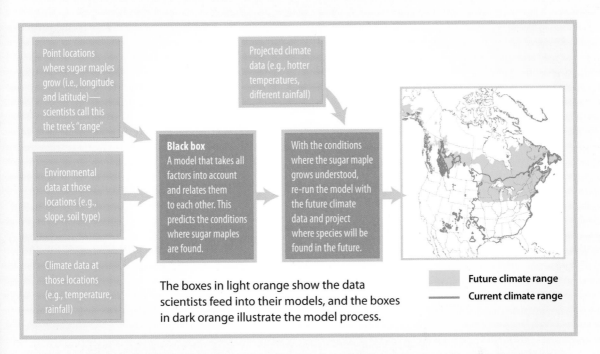

Point locations where sugar maples grow (i.e., longitude and latitude)— scientists call this the tree's "range"

Projected climate data (e.g., hotter temperatures, different rainfall)

Environmental data at those locations (e.g., slope, soil type)

Black box
A model that takes all factors into account and relates them to each other. This predicts the conditions where sugar maples are found.

With the conditions where the sugar maple grows understood, re-run the model with the future climate data and project where species will be found in the future.

Climate data at those locations (e.g., temperature, rainfall)

The boxes in light orange show the data scientists feed into their models, and the boxes in dark orange illustrate the model process.

Future climate range
Current climate range

scientists can confidently use them to analyze future scenarios. They can "add" greenhouse gases virtually, in different amounts, and project the effects on rainfall, oceans, and more 50 or 100 years from now.

Scientists also test the models against nature's own climate experiments. One major test involved the Philippine volcano Mount Pinatubo. It erupted in 1991, pouring huge amounts of particles into the atmosphere. The physics incorporated into the models said such dust should block the Sun and temporarily slow global warming— and that's just what happened.

In sum, climate models are not perfect representations of the world. However, internationally recognized climate models are the best available substitute. As climate modelers gain more experience, and have the benefit of better data, their models keep getting more sophisticated, and their projections of future climate become more and more reliable.

Simulating the Future Climate modelers take measurements of the current climate, add projections of future greenhouse-gas emissions, and put it all into computer models that incorporate the chemistry and physics of the atmosphere, land, and ocean to project future climate.

What's the best way to provide people with information about climate change?

There are many ways that people can benefit from having information about climate change, including being able to make informed policy and management decisions. This is one reason why people are talking about creating a national climate service. So, what functions would a national climate service provide?

A good place to start is with an organization that has a similar name and purpose—the National Weather Service, a government agency that was established in the late 1800s. The importance of the Weather Service is almost too obvious to mention. Without accurate reports about the current weather and predictions of future weather, planes would fly into thunderstorms unawares, ships would plow directly into hurricanes and typhoons, and people wouldn't know about blizzards barreling down on them. Also, planning for pretty much any outdoor activity

would become a lot more difficult. Without good weather forecasts, the losses in economic terms and in human lives would be huge.

Climate change unfolds on a slower scale—over decades rather than in hours. But now that we know it's happening, the need for forecasting how climate change will impact us has become clear as well. Knowing how much sea level is likely to rise, and how quickly, is crucial to knowing how to protect coastal areas from increased damage. Knowing how hurricane frequency and strength might change could affect building codes and evacuation strategies. Knowing how the intensity and frequency of droughts and heat waves might change would help city and regional planners manage water resources and mitigate threats to local economies.

The knowledge that these changes will come mostly from an increase in atmospheric levels of greenhouse gases could inform decisions about how to produce and use energy, and whether to develop alternative energy and other green technologies. If the world decides that limiting climate change is a priority, then this green technology could be an economic boon to the countries that perfect it.

Realizing that businesses, local governments, and individuals need the most reliable forecasts possible of how, when, and where the climate is likely to change, and what the impacts might be, universities, government agencies, and private companies have come together over the past year or so to figure out how such an entity might operate—how it would organize information and how it would deliver that information in the most useful way.

Delivering Climate Information Jane Lubchenco, Administrator of the National Oceanic and Atmospheric Administration, testifies before Congress.

What is *clean coal*?

Clean coal isn't a type of coal. It's a way of burning coal that could help slow down global warming—someday. It's not commercially available now, but it might be in a decade or two.

The reason scientists and energy companies are so interested in clean coal is that it may be the only way that we can continue to use coal long into the future without making the global warming problem worse. Some people want to stop using coal altogether, but others want to keep using it because there's much more of it in the world than there is oil or natural gas—enough to last hundreds of years. Coal is also cheaper today than any other fossil fuel. And unlike some renewable energy sources, like wind or photovoltaic solar, you can make electricity from coal day or night, windy or calm, and just about anywhere in the country.

It sounds perfect. But coal is also the dirtiest fossil fuel, in three different ways. First, the land and water near coal mines is significantly disturbed by some types of mining practices. Second, burning coal the way we do today leaves behind massive piles of toxic ash, and contributes to air pollution. Finally, burning coal puts lots of carbon dioxide, or CO_2, into the air. It's a special kind of pollutant because it's the major cause of global warming. Coal emits more CO_2 per unit of energy it provides than either oil or natural gas.

To keep that from happening, scientists have figured out ways to capture CO_2 from coal plants so that it doesn't get released into the air. They also know how to pump the CO_2 deep underground in places where they believe it can stay safely for hundreds or even thousands of years. The whole process is called CCS, or "Carbon Capture and Storage" (or "Sequestration," which means the same thing). When people talk about clean coal, that's usually what they mean. Different types of CCS technologies can also help reduce toxic ash and air pollution, in addition to reducing CO_2. None of them, however, can change the need for mining coal.

There are a couple of problems with CCS, though. First, capturing and storing the CO_2 adds costs. Second, while scientists and engineers are pretty confident that underground storage will work, it's a complex process, and we can't be certain that everything will work as planned until it's tried on a big scale. If the CO_2 just leaks out again, you haven't accomplished much. Many large-scale tests are scheduled over the next five to ten years to figure all this out.

If clean coal does work, it will mean higher costs for electricity, but that's true for all low-carbon electricity. And it could eventually play a large part in fighting global warming.

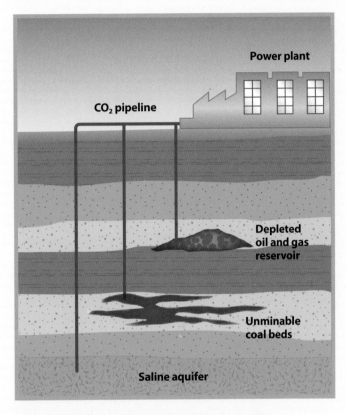

Carbon Capture and Storage The exhaust from burning coal can be cleaned of carbon dioxide, or CO_2, before it escapes; the CO_2 can then be piped deep underground.

Q How can we reduce the amount of greenhouse gases that humans emit?

A

Changing the way we make and use energy is an enormous challenge that will take decades, and a lot of resources and willpower, to accomplish.

What level of resources? It's hard to say for sure, but the Stern Review, a well-respected recent study on the economics of climate change, says it could cost as much as $2 trillion per year to stave off the worst effects of climate change by the year 2050. That's a huge number—but inaction is likely to cost even more. According to the Intergovernmental Panel on Climate Change, or IPCC, climate models suggest that if we keep burning fossil fuels on a "business-as-usual" basis, people around the world will experience dislocations for which the economic, environmental, and human costs will be huge.

Sea-level rise projected by the climate models would require relocating whole cities, which would be costly. Providing water to the estimated 500 million people whose supplies would fall below sustainable thresholds would

be costly. Feeding the world's population, as changing weather patterns put severe pressure on agriculture, would be costly. Based on the Stern Review, it is estimated that by the year 2050 the cost of adapting to climate change could be anywhere from $10 to $40 trillion per year.

The year 2050 seems far in the future, so it's tempting to delay action on climate change for a while. Unfortunately, the longer we wait to start, the more expensive it will be. It's kind of like losing weight—if your goal is to get down to 150 pounds, it's a lot easier if you start dieting when you weigh 160 pounds rather than wait until you weigh 220 pounds. The same goes for climate change—it's easier, and cheaper in the long run, to tackle the problem before it gets too far out of hand.

Fortunately, there are ways of slowing the rate at which we add greenhouse gases to the atmosphere that actually save money. These are familiar ideas like switching to more efficient cars, heating and air conditioning systems, light bulbs, and appliances; and putting better insulation in homes and buildings. But these actions can only take us so far. To reduce emissions of heat-trapping greenhouse gases to a relatively safe level, experts on the economics of energy and climate believe we'll have to do much more—like make a transition from the extensive use of fossil fuels to using lots more wind and solar energy. And, if we continue to use fossil fuels to generate electricity, then we must capture and sequester—that is, bury—the greenhouse gas emissions.

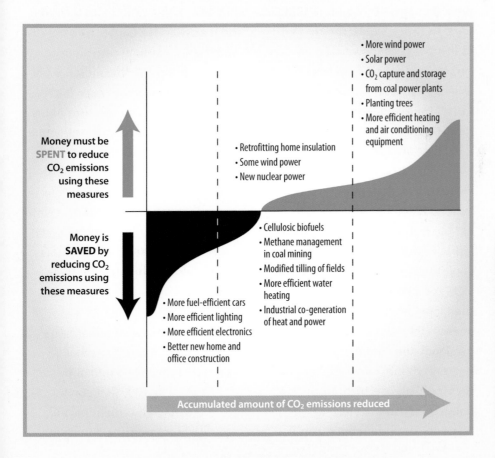

The Cost of Some Ways to Reduce CO₂ Emissions in the U.S. Some measures to reduce greenhouse gas emissions will actually save money. But to reach large enough reductions in emissions to avoid the worst effects of climate change will require also pursuing measures that will cost more.

What is your carbon footprint?

Defining *carbon footprint* is easy. It's the amount of carbon (in the form of carbon dioxide, or CO_2) you send into the atmosphere in the process of living your life. The average American has a carbon footprint of about 20 metric tons of CO_2 every year. Europeans use about half as much, even though their standard of living is as high as ours. In India, where the standard of living is much lower, the average carbon footprint per person is less than 2 tons. If you look at the entire world, the average human has a footprint of about 5 ½ tons.

These are only averages, though. Your own carbon footprint will be more or less, depending on lots of factors. If you live where it doesn't get too hot or too cold, you'll use less energy than average to heat or cool your house, and generate less CO_2. A small house uses less energy than a big house. A house that's energy-efficient because it's well insulated and uses high-efficiency heating, cooling, and appliances, uses less than one without those features. If you live close to where you work or go to school, you'll use less energy on average than those who live far away (it also depends, of course, on whether you walk, bike, drive, or take public transportation, and if you drive, on what your car's mileage is).

Many of these things are hard to control, but if you want to reduce your carbon footprint to fight climate change, there are ways to do it anyway. No matter how big or small your house is, for example, you can lower the thermostat a few degrees in winter and raise it a few in summer. You can turn out lights more often, and use more efficient bulbs, like compact fluorescents, wherever possible. You can make sure your next car gets higher mileage than your last car. You can use recycled products, and recycle more yourself, since it takes more energy to make new things from scratch than to make them from old things. And so on.

Unfortunately, there are aspects of your carbon footprint that you have much less control over. Take cars. The CO_2 that comes from burning gasoline is part of your carbon footprint. But so is

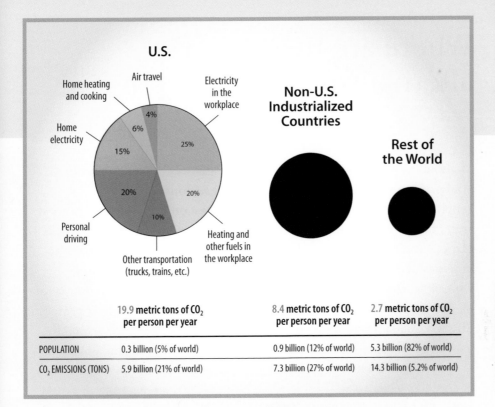

	19.9 **metric tons of CO$_2$** per person per year	8.4 **metric tons of CO$_2$** per person per year	2.7 **metric tons of CO$_2$** per person per year
POPULATION	0.3 billion (5% of world)	0.9 billion (12% of world)	5.3 billion (82% of world)
CO$_2$ EMISSIONS (TONS)	5.9 billion (21% of world)	7.3 billion (27% of world)	14.3 billion (5.2% of world)

Average Per-Capita CO$_2$ Emissions from Fossil Fuels in 2005 The U.S. emits lots more carbon per person than the rest of the world; it also emits more than other developed countries.

the energy used to make the car, and so is the energy used to make or mine the steel, plastic, and glass it's built from. So is the energy it takes to get the car from the factory to the dealer. So is your share of the energy it takes to build and maintain the roads you drive on. When it comes to electricity, you might have little control over where it comes from. Some ways of generating it (nuclear, wind, solar) are almost carbon-free. Others, like burning coal, are huge carbon dioxide generators.

In most cases, these contributors to carbon footprint are beyond our personal control.

In order to make major reductions in the average American's carbon footprint, therefore, it will take not just individual action, but action on a large scale by companies and by the government.

Finally, a word of warning— read the fine print on carbon footprints. Sometimes the footprint "weighs" the full molecule of CO$_2$, which is what was done in the lead paragraph above, and sometimes only the C (carbon) in the CO$_2$. To get the weight of the CO$_2$ from the weight of the C in the CO$_2$, you would need to multiply by $^{44}/_{12}$, so read the fine print.

Q Where are the nation's alternative-energy hotspots?

A The sources of fuels we use to power cars and trucks, heat homes, generate electricity, and so on, aren't distributed around the planet equally. Oil is most abundant in places like Saudi Arabia, Russia, Venezuela, and Iran. Coal is plentiful in the U.S., China, and Russia. Canada has substantial natural gas resources.

It's the same with alternative energy, like wind, solar, hydroelectric, biomass, and tidal energy. Within the U.S., the best source of wind is a wide belt that stretches from north to south across the center of the country, from Texas to North Dakota where it blows hardest and most steadily.

For solar power, you want a place where it's sunny a lot of the time. Ideally, you also want a location where the Sun is nearly overhead, so the sunlight doesn't hit the ground at an angle and spread out its energy. That makes the southern half of the country the best bet. And because the Sun shines most consistently in the desert, the best spots of all are places like New Mexico and Arizona.

Not only are these areas good sources of wind and solar, but they also have fewer people who would be disrupted by large-scale energy generation. But it also means that the electricity would have to be transported to population centers far away. That would require a whole new system of power lines. Another drawback with these energy sources, no matter what the location, is that they're variable. The Sun doesn't shine at night, and even in the desert it's sometimes cloudy. In windy spots, the wind doesn't always blow steadily.

Another form of renewable energy is geothermal—the heat from places where molten rock comes relatively close to the surface. Iceland, which has many volcanoes, gets most of its power this way. In the U.S., the hotspots are in California, Nevada, Utah, Wyoming, and Hawaii, and all of these but Wyoming have geothermal power plants.

Hydroelectric power is most abundant in mountainous areas like the Appalachian, Rocky, Cascade, and Sierra Nevada mountains. But those areas don't have many more places to build dams capable of generating lots of electricity. Conservationists argue that dams ruin river ecosystems, and some dams are actually being destroyed to restore free-flowing rivers.

Finally, there's biomass—plant matter that can either be burned directly or converted into fuels like ethanol. The biomass hotspots are the places where farmland and woodlands are most productive. It is important to compare how much energy it takes to grow and process biomass with the amount of energy you get out of it. It is the net energy that is important, and in some cases—like corn ethanol—it takes substantial energy to produce the fuel in the first place.

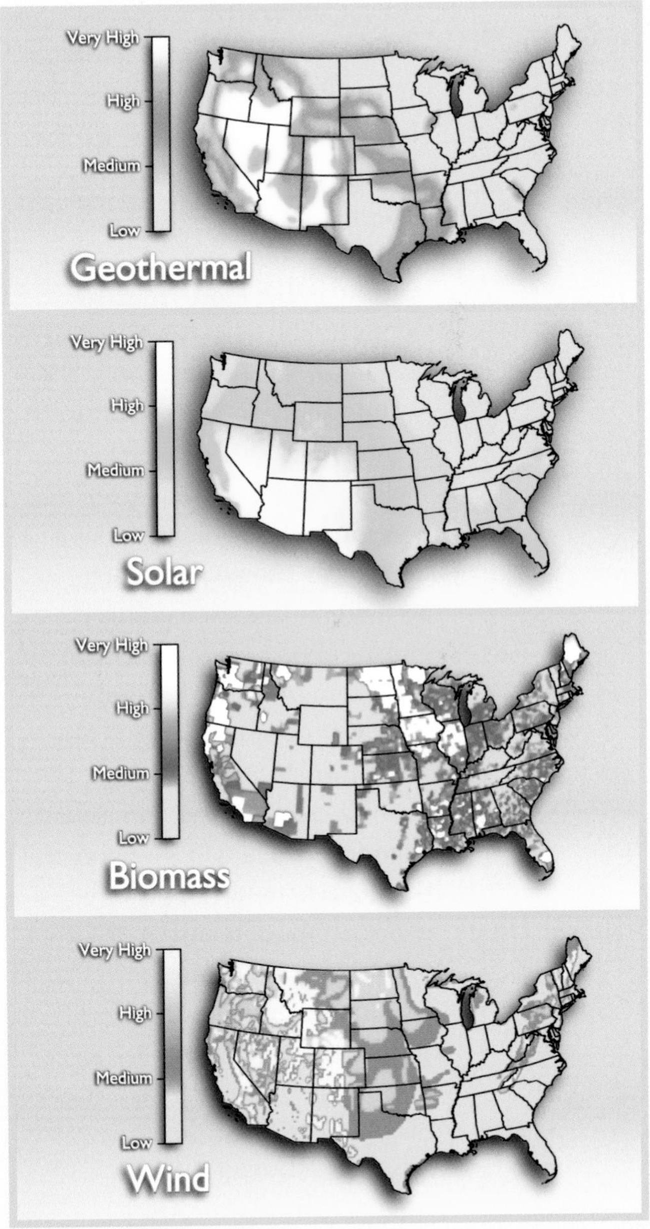

Geothermal

Solar

Biomass

Wind

Alternative Energy Hotspots These maps show where four types of alternative energy are most plentiful.

Q

What is the relationship between the energy we use today and climate?

A

The relationship between the energy we use today and Earth's climate depends on the source of the energy. People use energy for heating, for transportation, for lighting, for manufacturing, for communication, and for growing and harvesting food.

By far the most common way to produce that energy today is to burn fossil fuels like coal, oil, and natural gas (they're called fossil fuels because they come from the decomposed remains of ancient life, mostly plants). Fossil fuels account for the vast majority of global energy use. Burning (or, to use a more scientific term, *oxidation*) releases energy. It also releases waste gases into the atmosphere. That's why we have chimneys and tailpipes—because if these gases couldn't escape they'd choke off the combustion (to say nothing of choking us).

Among those waste gases is carbon dioxide, or CO_2. It's a greenhouse gas, meaning it traps heat rather than letting the heat escape into outer space. Before the Industrial Revolution, the human race wasn't burning enough of anything to make much of a difference. Since then, we've learned to use coal, oil, and natural gas and we've been using a lot more machinery. That requires a lot more energy, which means a lot more CO_2 in the atmosphere—there's already about 30 percent more of it now than there was before the Revolution, and the level is still rising. (A nearly sevenfold increase in world population since 1800 has also made a big difference).

The additional CO_2 that has accumulated in the atmosphere means that more heat is being trapped, which many thousands of scientists agree has already begun to affect the climate and will affect the climate even more as time goes on.

So that's the relationship between energy as we now produce it and climate. It's also why people are talking so much about

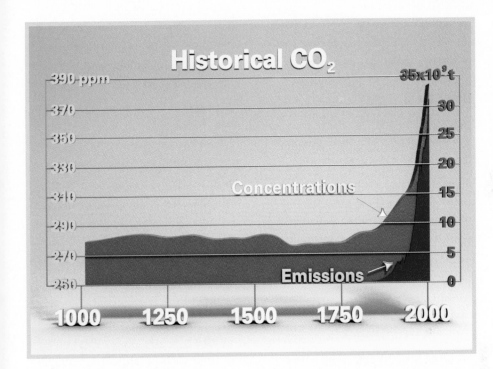

Historical CO$_2$

CO$_2$ Through the Ages
Carbon dioxide, or CO$_2$, emissions (measured in parts per million, or ppm) and CO$_2$ concentrations (measured in metric tons, or t) in the atmosphere began to rise when we began burning fossil fuels.

alternative kinds of energy that don't add to the greenhouse gases in the atmosphere. Wind turbines, solar energy arrays, nuclear power plants, and geothermal systems, are just a few examples. And coal plants that capture and store CO$_2$ before it escapes into the atmosphere may become a way to use some fossil fuel without changing the climate.

Such "low-carbon" energy will probably cost more than fossil fuel energy costs today. But some prominent economists have pointed that by using such low-carbon energy we could avoid much higher costs that are likely to be caused by global warming.

Q So how do we do something about the trends in global warming?

A It's too late to stop global warming, but we can limit its rise. From 1900 to 2005, says the Intergovernmental Panel on Climate Change, or IPCC, the planet's average surface temperature rose about .72°C (1.3°F)—and greenhouse gases, particularly CO_2, are very likely the explanation.

The IPCC report goes on to say that if people continue to force CO_2 to build up in the atmosphere by burning fossil fuels, cutting down forests and other activities, the planet will continue to warm.

Even if we could somehow keep emissions from growing, we'd still be pumping greenhouse gases into the atmosphere at a higher rate than any time in history—roughly 30 billion metric tons of CO_2 per year from fossil fuels, in addition to some non-CO_2 greenhouse gases. These gases would continue to build up in the atmosphere. That's because natural processes remove greenhouse gases from the atmosphere more slowly than we currently add them.

But what if we could stop CO_2 emissions completely instead of just keeping them from growing? Even then, the warming triggered by the gases we've already emitted could last for more than a thousand years. We wouldn't return to the temperatures and sea levels we've been accustomed to until after the year 3000.

So, the question is not how we stop warming, but rather how we limit it. There's a consensus among scientists that if the global average temperature rises 2°C (3.6°F) above the preindustrial temperature, there will be serious climate impacts. To stay under that limit, while allowing for economic growth in less-developed countries, industrialized countries like the U.S. would have to cut their carbon emissions some 80 percent by the year 2050, compared with 2005 levels, according to one commonly cited calculation. The world as a whole would have to cut carbon emissions by 50 percent overall. Some of that could come from using energy more efficiently—by using better home insulation, more efficient appliances, and cars that get much better gas mileage. That could get us large reductions, but not 80 percent.

To get that much, we'd have to change the way energy is produced.

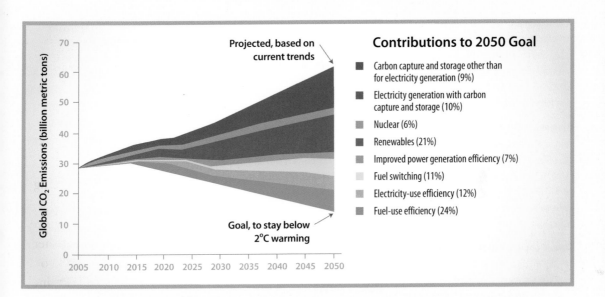

Contributions to 2050 Goal

- Carbon capture and storage other than for electricity generation (9%)
- Electricity generation with carbon capture and storage (10%)
- Nuclear (6%)
- Renewables (21%)
- Improved power generation efficiency (7%)
- Fuel switching (11%)
- Electricity-use efficiency (12%)
- Fuel-use efficiency (24%)

Projected, based on current trends

Goal, to stay below 2°C warming

Global CO_2 Emissions (billion metric tons)

Currently, the U.S. gets 85 percent of its energy from CO_2-emitting coal, oil, and natural gas and 15 percent from non-fossil sources like nuclear or renewables. We would need to reverse this equation. There's enough nuclear, wind, solar, hydroelectric, "clean coal"—where CO_2 is captured and stored underground—and other non-emitting energy to do this, especially if efficiency can reduce our total energy needs substantially. This, however, would require a huge change in our energy system—and it probably couldn't be done without higher costs for energy.

The only reason to spend a lot on fighting climate change would be if we think the cost of inaction would likely be even greater—and many economists believe just that. According to the Stern Review, a highly regarded analysis issued in 2006, doing nothing to reduce emissions could end up reducing the world's annual economic output by somewhere between 5 and 20 percent by 2050. The cost of staving off the worst effects, by contrast, would reduce annual economic activity by between 1 and 3.5 percent by 2050.

A Rainbow of Options for Cutting CO2
The upper edge of the rainbow represents projected emissions growth; the lower is where many scientists think we should be. The colored wedges show how we might get there.

Glossary

Anthropogenic Something that is caused by human activity. For example, climate varies due to natural causes, but most scientists are convinced that much of the increase in Earth's average temperature over the past half-century is anthropogenic.

Biomass Plant matter that is either burned directly for energy or converted into fuels like ethanol or diesel oil. Biomass can come in the form of plants, like corn or grasses, grown deliberately for energy production; it can also be waste left over from agriculture or forestry.

Carbon capture and storage Also known as CCS, this is a process whereby **carbon dioxide** is stripped from the exhaust from a coal-fired power plant before exiting the smokestack. The CO_2 is then pumped into water-bearing formations deep underground or undersea, where it dissolves in the water. CCS has been demonstrated on small scales, but needs further testing before it can be considered a reliable option for limiting CO_2 emissions.

Carbon cycle The natural cycling of carbon through the land, ocean, atmosphere, and living things. Carbon is stored on our planet in several major ways, (1) as organic molecules in living and dead organisms in the biosphere, (2) as carbon dioxide gas in the atmosphere, (3) as fossil fuels and sedimentary rock deposits, like limestone in the lithosphere, and (4) as dissolved carbon dioxide and as calcium carbonate shells in some marine organisms in the oceans. The global carbon cycle

operates on different time scales—from days to millions of years.

Carbon dioxide A molecule made up of one carbon atom and two oxygen atoms (and, therefore, also known as CO_2), CO_2 is generated by many natural processes, including plant and animal cell respiration, the decay of organic matter, and volcanic activity. It is also a byproduct of combustion—that is, burning—of wood, plant matter, natural gas, oil and coal, among other things. CO_2 in the atmosphere contributes to the **greenhouse effect**; and scientists agree the buildup of high levels of CO_2 from human activities, especially burning **fossil fuels**, is causing **global warming**.

Carbon footprint The amount of carbon (in the form of **carbon dioxide**, or CO_2) every person sends into the atmosphere in the process of living his or her life. Some aspects of a carbon footprint are relatively easy to quantify, since it's easy to measure how much energy one uses in heating or lighting a home, or how much gasoline one uses in driving. Other aspects—how much carbon is emitted in making and transporting the products we use, how much carbon is emitted in the course of heating and lighting workplaces or other shared spaces, and much more, are harder to measure for individuals. Since agriculture also contributes to carbon emissions, most of the food we eat is also part of our carbon footprint.

"Clean coal" The term refers not to a form of coal, but rather to a process in which

exhaust from a coal-fired power plant is stripped of **carbon dioxide** before exiting the smokestack. The presumption is that this CO_2 will then be pumped underground or undersea in a process known as **carbon capture and storage**, or **CCS**. This process does not remove other pollutants, including aerosols and sulfur dioxide, from coal exhaust.

Climate The long-term average conditions for a particular region. For example, the climate in the northeastern U.S. is warm in summer, cold in winter, with lots of snow in the mountains. The climate of Florida is hot and humid in summer, warm in winter with a relatively high risk of hurricanes.

Climate change The various changes in climate already seen and projected to increase as a result of **global warming**. Among them are rising sea level, increased intensity of storms, more frequent droughts and heat waves, and changes in the timing of seasons.

Drought The most familiar meaning is lower than average precipitation for a prolonged period. But this actually only describes meteorological drought. There's also hydrological drought, which is low water flow and low water levels in streams and rivers, and agricultural drought, which is low soil moisture. These can be related, and can occur all at once, in which case the term is environmental drought.

El Niño The appearance of unusually warm waters in the eastern Pacific Ocean.

Fossil fuels Fuels whose original source was organic matter—largely plants and microscopic animals—that were buried millions of years ago and gradually converted by underground heat and pressure into coal, crude oil, and natural gas.

Geothermal energy This term has two entirely different meanings. The first is heat from pockets of underground molten rock that lie relatively close to the surface, often in areas where there's volcanic activity. This subsurface energy can be tapped to heat homes and provide hot water. The other form of geothermal energy comes from much shallower depths of about 6.1 meters (20 feet) or so, where the temperature hovers at a constant 10°C (50°F) or so over much of the Earth. During winter in places where air temperatures fall much lower, this energy can be tapped for heat. In summer in places where the temperature rises much higher, the relatively cool earth can be used for cooling.

Global climate model This is a complex computer model that attempts to simulate the Earth's climate in order to understand how it changes over time. Also known as GCMs, global climate models can't be as complex as our actual planet, but have increased in sophistication as computers have become more powerful and as scientific understanding has grown. They have successfully reproduced past episodes of climate change, which gives scientists confidence about the models' projections of future changes.

Global warming In general, this is simply a sustained rise in the average temperature of the Earth, whatever the cause. In common usage today, the phrase refers to the current phase of warming that scientists widely agree is being caused in large part by **greenhouse gases** generated by human activity.

Greenhouse effect The trapping of heat by gases in the Earth's atmosphere.

More specifically, visible light from the Sun passes through the atmosphere and heats the Earth's surface. The warmed Earth then radiates **infrared radiation**, or heat, back toward space. So-called greenhouse gases, like carbon dioxide, absorb some of this infrared. This traps the heat instead of letting it escape into space, which ends up warming the atmosphere and the Earth's surface.

Greenhouse gases Sometimes abbreviated as GHG's, these are atmospheric gases that trap **infrared radiation** and thus contribute to the **greenhouse effect**. Among the many greenhouse gases are water vapor, **carbon dioxide**, **methane**, **nitrous oxide**, and the gases collectively known as halocarbons.

Hydroelectric power Electricity generated by the energy of flowing or falling water. The moving water drives a turbine, which generates electricity. Huge dams, like the Hoover Dam in Nevada and the dams spanning the Columbia River in the Pacific Northwest, were built in part to tap the energy of major rivers.

Ice age A period during which polar ice covers significantly more of the Earth's surface than it does today. Ice ages are caused by changes in Earth's orbit around the Sun and in the composition of gases in the atmosphere. Over the past 800,000 years or so, Earth has experienced eight major ice ages, lasting about 100,000 years, on average. Ice ages are separated by so-called interglacial periods, which last between 10,000 and 30,000 years, on average. The last Ice Age ended about 10,000 years ago.

Infrared radiation A form of electromagnetic radiation. Visible light, X-rays, ultraviolet light, and radio waves are other forms of electromagnetic (EM) radiation. Radio waves have the lowest energy and longest wavelengths, X-rays the highest energy and shortest wavelengths.

Infrared radiation has slightly longer wavelengths than visible light and slightly shorter wavelengths than radio waves. Different forms of EM radiation have an easier or harder time penetrating Earth's atmosphere. Infrared radiation is trapped by greenhouse gases like carbon dioxide, which warms the Earth in the **greenhouse effect**.

Light-emitting diode Also known as an LED, this technology creates light by running current through specially engineered solid-state materials similar to those used in computer chips. A light bulb using LED's is more efficient than a CFL bulb, and lasts even longer. It's also more expensive.

Methane One of the **greenhouse gases**. Methane comes from natural sources, including the decomposition of organic matter in swamps and from the digestive systems of termites. It also comes from agricultural sources, including manure from pigs, cows, and chickens; from the digestive systems of cows; and from the decomposition of organic matter in rice paddies. Methane is also present in undersea deposits known as methane clathrates.

Nitrous oxide A **greenhouse gas** generated as a byproduct of the combustion of fossil fuels and also generated in the manufacture of fertilizer.

Solar photovoltaic energy Electricity generated directly by sunlight falling on cells made of semiconductors. The sunlight triggers the release of electrons to form an electric current. This is the more familiar type of solar energy; rooftop solar arrays and the solar chargers that run calculators are examples of photovoltaic energy. In contrast, solar thermal energy is electricity generated by focusing sunlight on a fluid like oil, then using the hot fluid to heat water. The steam in turn drives a turbine, which generates electricity.

Weather The short-term (hourly, daily, weekly, or even monthly) variations in local temperature, precipitation, and humidity.

Index

Data Sources and Image Credits

Cover: NASA Goddard Space Flight Center Image by Reto Stöckli; enhancements by Robert Simmon; data and technical support: MODIS Land Group; MODIS Science Data Support Team; MODIS Atmosphere Group; MODIS Ocean Group; USGS EROS Data Center; USGS Terrestrial Remote Sensing Flagstaff Field Center; Defense Meteorological Satellite Program. P. 6: Based on *Intergovernmental Panel On Climate Change Fourth Assessment Report* (2007). PP. 8-9: Based on *Intergovernmental Panel On Climate Change Fourth Assessment Report* (2007). P. 10: Based on Stouffer, R.J., G. Hegerl, and S. Tett (2000): A Comparison of Surface Air Temperature Variability in Three 1000-Yr Coupled Ocean–Atmosphere Model Integrations. *J. Climate, 13*: 513–537. P. 11: Temperature data taken from Mann ME, Zhang Z, Hughes MK, Bradley RS, Miller SK, Rutherford S, and Ni F (2008). Proxy-based reconstructions of hemispheric and global surface temperature variations over the past two millennia. *PNAS, 105*: 13252-13257. Global CO_2 data from the Carbon Dioxide Information Analysis Center and Oak Ridge National Labs (http://cdiac.esd.ornl.gov/ftp/trends/co2/lawdome.smoothed.yr75). P. 12: NASA/The COMET Program. P. 15: Based on Doran PT and Zimmerman MK (2009). Examining the scientific consensus on climate change. *EOS, 90* (3): 22-23. P. 17: Based on Climate Research Unit, University of East Anglia/Hadley Center, UK Met Office and Jones, P.D., New, M., Parker, D.E., Martin, S. and Rigor, I.G. (1999): Surface air temperature and its variations over the last 150 years. *Reviews of Geophysics 37, 173-199.* P. 19: Courtesy Yavor Parashkevov. P. 21: Based on "Topeka WSFO Airport" station of the "Global Daily Climatology Network," administered by the National Climatic Data Center's Climate Services. P. 25: Based on *Intergovernmental Panel On Climate Change Fourth Assessment Report* (2007). P. 27: Based on Union of Concerned Scientists (http://www.climatechoices.org/ne/impacts_ne/climates.html). P. 29: Based on shoreline data and maps from the National Oceanic and Atmospheric Administration and digital elevation models from the U.S. Geological Survey. P. 31: Based on McKenney DW, Pedlar JH, Lawrence K, Campbell K, and Hutchinson MF (2007). Beyond traditional hardiness zones: using climate envelopes to map plant range limits. *BioScience, 57* (11): 929-937. P. 33: Courtesy House Committee on Science and Technology. P. 37: Based on J. Creyts, A. Derkach, S. Nyquist, K. Ostrowski, and J. Stephenson, *Reducing U.S. Greenhouse Gas Emissions: How Much at What Cost?* Executive Report of the U.S. Greenhouse Gas Abatement Mapping Initiative, McKinsey and Company, December 2007. P. 39: Based on Energy Information Administration, *Emissions of Greenhouse Gases in the United States 2007*, U.S. Department of Energy, Washington, DC, Dec. 2008; Population Reference Bureau, *World Population Data Sheet 2008*, www.prb.org; World Resources Institute, Climate Analysis Indicators Tool (CAIT) Version 6.0, http://cait.wri.org/. P. 41: Resource maps from the National Renewable Energy Laboratory (http://www.nrel.gov/gis/maps.html). P. 43: Global fossil-fuel CO_2 emissions as published by the Carbon Dioxide Information and Analysis Center (http://cdiac.ornl.gov/trends/emis/meth_reg.html). Atmospheric CO_2 concentrations as published in U.S. Global Change Research Program, *Climate Change Impacts on the United States: The Potential Consequences of Climate Variability and Change*, US Climate Change Science Program, updated August 2004. http://www.usgcrp.gov/usgcrp/Library/nationalassessment/2IntroB.pdf. P. 45: Based on International Energy Agency, *Energy Technology Perspectives 2008*, OECD, Paris, 2008.